Let All the Earth Praise!

Written and illustrated by

Isabella Theodora Cardwell

WestBow Press books may be ordered through booksellers or by contacting:

WestBow Press
A Division of Thomas Nelson & Zondervan
1663 Liberty Drive
Bloomington, IN 47403
www.westbowpress.com
844-714-3454

Because of the dynamic nature of the Internet, any web addresses or links contained in this book may have changed since publication and may no longer be valid. The views expressed in this work are solely those of the author and do not necessarily reflect the views of the publisher, and the publisher hereby disclaims any responsibility for them.

Any people depicted in stock imagery provided by Getty Images are models, and such images are being used for illustrative purposes only.
Certain stock imagery © Getty Images.

Interior Image Credit: Isabella Theodora Cardwell

ISBN: 978-1-6642-0093-7 (sc)
ISBN: 978-1-6642-0095-1 (hc)
ISBN: 978-1-6642-0094-4 (e)

Library of Congress Control Number: 2020914369

Print information available on the last page.

WestBow Press rev. date: 10/01/2020

WESTBOW
PRESS®
A DIVISION OF THOMAS NELSON
& ZONDERVAN

Foreword

It is an honor to endorse this book. Through colorful watercolor paintings, Bella provides an inspiring story of praise unto God that children can understand and interact with. And while it is geared towards children, adults and parents will also find it a useful tool for building relationships and interacting with children.

Dr. Greg Hackett, Senior Pastor,
The Bridge Community Church,
Warrenton, VA

Dedication

For God, my Savior, and my healer, Jesus Christ, who has breathed these pictures and words into my heart. I will continue to exalt Him with my life.

"O give thanks unto the Lord; for he is good: for his mercy endureth for ever." – Psalm 136:1KJV

Acknowledgements

I would like to thank Julia Heckathorn for showing me that God will do amazing things when we surrender our lives, our hearts, and all that we are to Him… God can use even a 13-year-old to write a children's book.

I would like to thank Betz Green, my art mentor, and friend, for opening up the world of art to me, and showing me the countless possibilities that come with art!!

I would like to thank Pastor Malik Abney, my Worship and Fine Arts pastor. He taught me the importance of praising, and showed me that when we praise, God is present with us, so everything upsetting from ourselves; anxiety, fear, and anger: leaves us as we offer God our full worship.

Sing praises to God!

Awake clouds, birds, and wind!

See God and rejoice!

Come sun,
river, and trees!

See God and
praise Him!

The wind sung
through the trees.

They whispered a
song of praise.

The trees and
the clouds
danced to their
song

while the world
came to life!

The great bows
of the trees awoke
the birds.

Their
wings beat,
and their
mouths sang!

They sang
with glory to
God!

Come, come out!
Bring light to the
world!

It cried out to God in a song of joy, and thanks giving!

The flowers saw the light, and opened up to receive its life!

They opened and
showed colors of
life and joy, and
sang together to
God!

All the earth, the footstool of God, sang, and danced, and worshipped God in the highest heaven!

So, with this, the earth
lifted its voice, and
honored Jesus.

So,
with this,
each morning,
the world glorifies God!

With each day, the world sings to God!

With
this, every
evening still,
the world
praises, and
sings!

So, if…

the wind,

the sun,

the trees,

The birds,

the rivers,

and the waters,

and

all the earth

praises God.

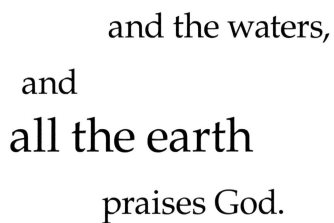

How much more should

we…

His children...

Cry out to Him in praise!

Printed in the United States
By Bookmasters